I0814472

THE POCKET MUSICALS

Published in 2025
by Gemini Books
Part of Gemini Books Group

Based in Woodbridge and London

Marine House, Tide Mill Way,
Woodbridge, Suffolk IP12 1AP
United Kingdom

www.geminibooks.com

Text by Roland Hall
Cover illustration by Natalie Floss

ISBN 978-1-80247-343-8

A CIP catalogue record for this book is available from the British Library.

Manufacturer's EU Representative: Eurolink Compliance Limited,
25 Herbert Place, Dublin, D02 AY86, Republic of Ireland.
admin@eurolink-europe.ie

Printed in China

10 9 8 7 6 5 4 3 2 1

Picture Credits:
Alamy Stock Photo: / Pictorial Press Ltd 4; / Collection Christophel 6; PictureLux / The Hollywood Archive 16; / Everett Collection Inc 118.
Adobe Stock Photo: 120, 121, 123, 125, 127.

THE POCKET

MUSICALS

G:

CONTENTS

INTRODUCTION

Musical movies are joyous, colourful, happy, moving, spectacular, thought-provoking – and more. The very best ones – and those are the ones this book is filled with – will leave you humming, singing and even dancing for days afterwards as you remember the great tunes and fabulous moves.

Admittedly, some are more serious than others, with gritty themes and perilous moments. Some feature nothing but singing. Some are more like movies with songs added to them. But the music is always an integral part of what makes the movie so interesting and enjoyable.

Whichever kind of musical it is – traditional or non-conformist, old or new – it doesn't really matter, as long as you are gripped, staring at the screen and tapping your hands (or feet). More recently, there has been a fashion for "jukebox" musicals, where a famous artist's work has a story built around it. *Mamma Mia!* is probably the most successful (and best!) example of this. It does not always work, but when it does, the results are magnificent.

"I was very influenced by musicals like *Singin' in the Rain* and *West Side Story.*"

— Director John Woo,
The Observer, 2000

"I seem to be drawn to things that actually happen."

— Vincente Minnelli, interview with Henry Sheehan, 1978

In the movie genre of musicals, the earliest ones tended to be filmed spectaculars of popular stage shows. The "new" technology of film (and then sound) of the 1930s meant that everyone was able to enjoy the amazing song and dance routines from the comfort of their local movie theatre, popcorn in hand.

And as the technology evolved, so did the movies, with expanding storylines and amazing scenery to match. Hollywood entered a golden era of musicals in the '50s, and lengthy, technicolor spectaculars became the order of the day; many were truly amazing, and examples include *An American in Paris, Singin' in the Rain* and *The King and I.*

These days, stage shows are still adapted and filmed for the big screen, but also the reverse happens: big movies end up on stage, wowing audiences in the West End and Broadway alike. And even the streaming giants have got in on the act, the last movie in this book, *Emilia Pérez,* was released in theatres shortly before broadcast by Netflix...

And the musicals keep coming. The sheer volume, quality and diversity of content speaks for itself: people love musicals! And why wouldn't they? Allowing expression of all sorts of feelings, exploring all kinds of (sometimes quite serious) subjects in a fun manner is great. But above all, it's just fun to be able to sing (and dance) along to your favourite tunes.

"I went from being a fan of musicals to writing musicals when I saw that show."

— Lin-Manuel Miranda on *Rent*, interview with Terry Gross, NPR, 2020

THE GLAMOUR FACTOR

There is a "glamour factor" listed in the reviews that follow. It is simply an indicator of how spectacular or glamorous a movie is. The most simple stories – films with a perhaps serious subject and a few tunes – will score a 1. Full-blown, all-singing, all-dancing extravaganzas will score 5. So put on your dancing shoes and get ready to sing!

"It's true, I didn't want to be a dancer."

— Gene Kelly at the American Film Institute, quoted by Paul Rosenfield, *Los Angeles Times*, 1985

50 MUST-SEE MUSICALS

① The Wizard of Oz, 1939

Director: Victor Fleming
Runtime: 102 mins
Glamour factor: 5/5

If you have yet to see *The Wizard of Oz,* you must drop everything (this book included) and find a way to see it, right now. Done? That's good, you can see why. Now, it may be the first entry in this book, but it is easily one of the best musicals ever made – heck, it is one of the best movies ever made, full stop!

What makes it so magical and unmissable? The visuals transport the viewer from black-and-white Kansas to technicolor Oz. The surreal story is meaningful and moving (there's even a moral at the end), the songs are stellar – 'Over the Rainbow' won the Best Song Academy Award – and the sentiment simply sublime. Now go watch it again...

"A heart is ... judged by how much you are loved by others."

– The Wizard (to the Tin Man)

"I can't believe it. Right here where we live – right here in St. Louis!"

— Esther Smith

② Meet Me in St. Louis, 1944

Director: Vincente Minnelli
Runtime: 113 mins
Glamour factor: 4/5

Judy Garland is back and director Minnelli liked her so much he married her after the two met on set. Their daughter? Liza Minnelli (who we'll see later).

Meet Me in St. Louis is a happy little slice-of-life rom-com based around the Smith family from St. Louis. Filled with excitement at the thought of the upcoming World Fair, daughter Esther (Garland) is in love with John (Tom Drake), the boy next door, and her sister Rose, the eldest, is hopeful of a romance, too. Domestic dreams are shattered when Mr. Smith announces the family will be moving to New York City the next year. Can the Smiths enjoy Christmas with such turmoil going on? The singing of 'Have Yourself a Merry Little Christmas' would suggest a yes.

Despite its simple premise and seemingly everyday characters, this musical delivers a meaningful moral and a happy ending.

③ Singin' in the Rain, 1952

Director: Gene Kelly
Runtime: 103 mins
Glamour factor: 5/5

It was only 1952 and already Hollywood was making movies about Hollywood. *Singin' in the Rain* involves the machinations of Don Lockwood (Gene Kelly), his fellow movie star Lina (Jean Hagen), who is in love with him, and the actress Kathy (Debbie Reynolds). The quartet is completed by his old friend Cosmo (Donald O'Connor). They get up to all sorts (including singing in the rain) over a series of truly stunning song and dance numbers that showcase absolutely the best that Hollywood had to offer.

Part homage to silent movies and part love story, it is wholly a glorious celebration of talkies, colour, living life and fun. *Singin' in the Rain* is a technicolor feast for the eyes and a treat for the ears: unmissable.

"Lina. She can't act, she can't sing, she can't dance. A triple threat."

— Cosmo

④ Gentlemen Prefer Blondes, 1953

Director: Howard Hawks
Runtime: 91 mins
Glamour factor: 5/5

To be honest, *Gentlemen Prefer Blondes* is almost worth watching just for Marilyn Monroe's jaw-dropping rendition of 'Diamonds are a Girl's Best Friend'. But you need to see the whole thing to fully appreciate what's on show. Marilyn, yes, but also the music, the script, the scenery, the cast – it all meshes together in the most exquisite manner.

Lorelei (Monroe) and her best friend Dorothy (Jane Russell) are showgirls who aspire to something more. For the former it's a rich husband, for the latter it's a guy who is nice to her (and handsome!). Lorelei plans to wed her rich boyfriend Gus (Tommy Noonan), and the two women travel to France, accompanied anonymously by a private investigator (Elliott Reid), hired by the suspicious husband-to-be. Two guys, two gals. A whole lot of confusion and some singing later, this delightful musical roars to its logical conclusion; it's brilliant.

“You *do* wear it on your head. I just *love* finding new places to wear diamonds.”

— Lorelei Lee

“To flee or not to flee, that is the question.”

— Slug

⑤ Kiss Me Kate, 1953

Director: George Sidney
Runtime: 109 mins
Glamour factor: 5/5

There are a few things about *Kiss Me Kate* that grate with a modern audience. Based on Shakespeare's ever-popular but increasingly problematic *The Taming of the Shrew*, you only need look at the film poster to wonder if it is even real: Howard Keel is spanking Kathryn Grayson, who is bent over his arm.

So far, so bad. However, the good news is that there is also plenty right with *Kiss Me Kate.* Certain aspects of the storyline may be – how shall I put it – slightly old-fashioned, but the (Cole Porter) songs are brilliant (it's got 'Too Darn Hot' in it for a start; and 'Brush Up on your Shakespeare' is a real hidden gem) and the side plots and subtexts are fascinating, driving in ever more frantic manner to the inevitable, glorious climax.

⑥ Carmen Jones, 1954

Director: Otto Preminger
Runtime: 105 mins
Glamour factor: 2/5

Opera fans among you will have noticed the presence of "Carmen" in the title, and it does indeed relate to Georges Bizet's 1875 opera of that name. *Carmen* is a tragedy and *Carmen Jones* certainly follows that line.

In North Carolina in the USA during World War II, Carmen Jones (Dorothy Dandridge) works in a factory. She has a reputation, and it's not good. She is arrested for fighting and is to be accompanied to the authorities some distance away by newly betrothed soldier Joe (Harry Belafonte). She decides to seduce him – and when he spurns her advances she redoubles her efforts. I won't be giving much away to say that it all ends in tears.

Carmen Jones is a hugely significant film, not least because it was one of the first to feature such a large African-American cast. A true original, it is deservedly preserved in the US's National Film Registry.

"That don't give you no right to own me!"

— Carmen Jones

⑦ Seven Brides for Seven Brothers, 1954

Director: Stanley Donen
Runtime: 102 mins
Glamour factor: 1/5

First off, I'm going to tell you that *Seven Brides for Seven Brothers* won the Best Scoring of a Musical Picture so you know that the music is brilliant. It would have won more (four nominations) but for a certain *On the Waterfront.*

It is 1850, and "unsophisticated" backwoodsman Adam (Howard Keel) ventures into town where he finds a bride, Milly (Jane Powell), and brings her back to his remote cabin. It turns out he has six brothers, all just as "unsophisticated" as he is, and Milly will be taking care of all of them. Milly is not at all in agreement and, after helping them socialize and – to cut a long story short(er) – they kidnap six women (uh oh). This being the movies, it's OK in the end and nobody comes to harm or is arrested for false imprisonment. *Seven Brides...* is actually a superb example of last-century Americana.

"Pa used to say love is kind of like the measles!"

— Adam

⑧ Guys and Dolls, 1955

Director: Joseph L. Mankiewicz
Runtime: 150 mins
Glamour factor: 3/5

One of the big movies from Hollywood's 1950s golden era of musicals, *Guys and Dolls* is high on the list of all-time classics. Why, I bet there's even a production on somewhere near you, wherever you are, as it is still one of the most popular musicals around.

It's an impressive cast: the guys are Sky Masterson (Marlon Brando) and Nathan Detroit (Frank Sinatra); the gals are Sister Sarah Brown (Jean Simmons) and Miss Adelaide (Vivian Blaine, reprising her role from Broadway). The story is one of redemption, ultimately, for Sky and Nathan, both gamblers who (eventually) see the error of their ways.

Guys and Dolls scooped four Academy Awards, including Art Direction, Cinematography and Costume Design: 'I'll Know' it makes sense!

"A guy doesn't wanna feel that he's just like a piece of material a woman'll cut up and sew."

— Sky Masterson

"I wanted to marry her when I saw the moonlight shining on the barrel of her father's shotgun."

— Ali Hakim

⑨ Oklahoma!, 1955

Director: Fred Zinnemann
Runtime: 148 mins
Glamour factor: 3/5

Another musical from the magical partnership of Rodgers & Hammerstein, *Oklahoma!* is a slice of good old-fashioned Americana, and highly entertaining to boot.

In a storyline that is highly reminiscent of a modern rom-com, Curly (Gordon MacRae) is a cowboy who hopes to marry Laurey (Shirley Jones), his secret love. Unfortunately, her father doesn't like cowboys. To make matters worse, Curly and Laurey are blessed with the communication skills of the cattle he looks after, so they spend most of the film in a state of mutual misunderstanding. There's a baddie, Jud (Rod Steiger), plenty of fightin' – and a love triangle, too.

Oklahoma! is a homage to a lost America, and is magnificent fun.

⑩ The King and I, 1956

Director: Walter Lang
Runtime: 133 mins
Glamour factor: 5/5

This is one of a number of Rodgers & Hammerstein-penned (*see page 120*) musicals in this book. The two are legends of musical theatre – and by extension – musical movies. *The King and I* was a multi-award winner and a huge success globally.

The musical is based (loosely) on a true story: schoolteacher Anna (Deborah Kerr) goes to Bangkok to tutor the children of King Mongkut (Yul Brynner). Her relationship with the king is somewhat fractious, involving discussion of manners, relationships and civilization, among other matters. Interesting adventures ensue, and there is, of course, a love story at the film's heart. There is also an interesting comparison of cultures, and empire and imperialism, too.

It's a curious film by modern standards, but the sheer spectacle and musical numbers are still very impressive.

"Death is not worse pain than an empty life."

— Lun Tha

⑪ West Side Story, 1961 and 2021

Director: Robert Wise and Jerome Robbins/Steven Spielberg
Runtime: 152/156 mins
Glamour factor: 5/5

One of the biggest and best, *West Side Story* was a groundbreaking film when it came out and has been influential ever since. It is based on the Shakespeare play *Romeo and Juliet*, but only loosely, as it involves New York gangs the Jets and the Sharks. Maria (Natalie Wood), sister of one of the leaders of the Sharks, falls for Tony (Richard Beymer), a former member of the Jets. It starts badly, racial tension is rife, and it all goes horribly wrong. In between are some of the most spectacular song and dance sequences on celluloid, with the city heat and youthful energy combining to make explosive, compulsive viewing.

There was a 2021 remake, directed by Spielberg. The result was slicker, louder and more colourful. Both are worth viewing, but the original remains one of the best musical movies of all time (11 Academy Awards!).

"All of you! You all killed him... Not with bullets, or guns, with hate."

— Maria

"As I expected: 'Mary Poppins, practically perfect in every way'."

— Mary Poppins

⑫ Mary Poppins, 1964

Director: Robert Stevenson
Runtime: 139 mins
Glamour factor: 4/5

Musicals can be sweet, touching, funny, moving or meaningful. Sometimes, they can be all of the above, and that is the case with *Mary Poppins*, an absolute barnstorming (chimney-sweeping?) smash.

The incredible Julie Andrews plays the title role, a nanny who, literally, drops out of the sky to take care of the unruly-but-nice-really Banks children. Various encounters with Mary's family and acquaintances ensue, most notably her friend Bert (Dick Van Dyke and his awful-but-charming cockney accent). He transports them into a picture, and is also the lead behind one of the musical highlights: 'Step in Time'. There are many more fantastic songs, including 'A Spoonful of Medicine' and 'Feed the Birds', before Mary has to move on.

Sixty years on this film is still magical, and, of course, supercalifragilisticexpialidocious!

"The difference between a lady and a flower girl is not how she behaves, but how she is treated."

— Eliza Doolittle

⑬ My Fair Lady, 1964

Director: George Cukor
Runtime: 173 mins
Glamour factor: 4/5

Into the 1960s, musicals were getting longer, but that was not a problem, because the standard remained high. Nearly three hours long, *My Fair Lady* offered quality and quantity in equal measure. Audrey Hepburn plays Eliza Doolittle, a flower girl with a coarse cockney accent. Fortunately, she overhears linguist Henry Higgins (Rex Harrison) boast how he could teach her to speak such good English she'd be able to pass for a duchess. The bet is accepted and the lessons start.

After a not-so-subtle look at the class struggle and the battle of the sexes, Eliza's hard work pays off and she is, indeed, taken for a princess, albeit by another imposter. But where does Eliza fit in now: with high society, the middle classes or back home? This superb, hilarious rom-com, based on the George Bernard Shaw play *Pygmalion*, provides all the answers.

⑭ The Umbrellas of Cherbourg, 1964

Director: Jacques Demy
Runtime: 91 mins
Glamour factor: 5/5

This is a film like no other. In the style of opera, or stage musicals, there is no dialogue, everything is sung to a brilliant jazz soundtrack written by Michel Legrand. The sets and costumes are jaw-dropping and almost glow, such is the amazing saturation of the colour. And the story...

Guy (Nino Castelnuovo) and Geneviève (Catherine Deneuve) are a young couple in love, but he has to leave for military service. She gets pregnant on his last night in Cherbourg, but they lose touch over his time away. Both move on and marry others, but are reunited in the denouement, one of the most painfully beautiful scenes ever filmed.

An absolute feast for eyes and ears, the film was a big influence on Damien Chazelle's *La La Land* and when you see it, you'll know why.

"For all the young lovers of the world."

— Film poster tag line

⑮ The Sound of Music, 1965

Director: Robert Wise
Runtime: 174 mins
Glamour factor: 3/5

This is the big one. Possibly the most famous musical movie ever. The songs from *The Sound of Music* are national treasures, and make up an important part of the cultural fabric of America, as well as further afield. *The Sound of Music* tours in Austria are as popular today as they ever have been.

But why? It's a film, based very loosely on a true story, about a nun (Julie Andrews) who leaves the convent and decides to teach a group of children. She falls in love with their father (Christopher Plummer). But there is so much more to *The Sound of Music*... Every song is a singalong classic, every number utterly mesmerizing, and every scene brilliantly constructed. From 'The Sound of Music' to 'Climb Ev'ry Mountain', you probably know them all already. But that won't stop you from watching it again, will it?

"You brought music back into the house. I had forgotten."

— Captain Von Trapp

"Hello, gorgeous."

— Fanny Brice

⑯ Funny Girl, 1968

Director: William Wyler
Runtime: 149 mins
Glamour factor: 2/5

Musicals were still flying high at the tail end of the '60s, and *Funny Girl* was the latest in a long line of adaptations from stage to screen. It is ostensibly the story of Fanny Brice, the famous Hollywood actress, but it is ultimately the love story of Fanny and her husband Nicky. Barbra Streisand plays the part of Brice, reprising her role from the original Broadway production, and Omar Sharif plays Nicky, the gambler and loser.

The film is one long flashback, detailing the events throughout the life of Fanny, and much time is spent on her time with Nicky. Glamorous at first, things go downhill, and Nicky ultimately ends up in jail. But there are many superb musical numbers, the most famous of which is undoubtedly the gloriously executed 'Don't Rain on My Parade' in its colourful, lilting glory. If you ever wondered what the fuss was about Barbra Streisand, watch this and you'll understand.

⑰ Oliver!, 1968

Director: Carol Reed
Runtime: 153 mins
Glamour factor: 3/5

We've seen plenty of musicals based on the works of Shakespeare and other writers. This time it is the turn of Charles Dickens to provide the source material. Who would have thought that the miserable tale of an orphan, published in 1838, would make such a successful musical movie? It won the Best Picture and Best Director Academy Awards in 1969, among many others.

Orphan Oliver Twist (Mark Lester) lives in a workhouse but escapes to London, where eventually he ends up in the clutches of Fagin (Ron Moody), who controls a gang of wayward children. Nasty Bill Sikes (Oliver Reed) and his nice girlfriend Nancy (Shani Wallis) are also involved as the action unfolds on the grubby streets of the capital. This may not seem like jolly, happy singing material, but the songs in *Oliver!* are fantastic, and performed to perfection by a really superb cast: 'Please sir, can we have some more?'

"We must have civil words, Bill. Civil words."

— Fagin

⑱ Fiddler on the Roof, 1971

Director: Norman Jewison
Runtime: 181 mins
Glamour factor: 4/5

Great musical content can come from the most surprising sources, and the problems of a milkman in early twentieth-century Russia certainly fits that category. But what a musical it is: three hours of beautiful, haunting songs, stunning locations and, of course, superb routines.

One reason for its high acclaim and popularity with the general public is the many serious themes that pervade throughout *Fiddler on the Roof*, from Jewish struggles and poverty to arranged marriages and love. The easy-going nature of the film is clear from the start when Tevye (Topol) breaks the fourth wall and addresses the audience.

Ahead of its time, amazing, political and thought-provoking, this lengthy film is an absolute masterpiece.

"Without our traditions, our lives would be as shaky as ... as ... as a *fiddler* — on the roof!"

— Tevye

⑲ Willy Wonka & the Chocolate Factory, 1971

Director: Mel Stuart
Runtime: 100 mins
Glamour factor: 4/5

The original book *Charlie and the Chocolate Factory* by Roald Dahl has been filmed various times, usually with songs, but this is the original and best version. Gene Wilder is a revelation as the beyond eccentric factory owner of the title, and his casual indifference to events around him is brilliantly portrayed.

Charlie Bucket (Peter Ostrum) lives in poverty with Grandpa Joe (Jack Albertson) and other relations. He dreams of winning one of the Golden Tickets, hidden in Wonka bars, that grant entry to the secretive chocolate factory. He manages to procure one and starts his tour, accompanied by the other, ungrateful, winners. One by one they are picked off...

There are fantastic sights and sounds galore, tons of sweets, and memorable music aplenty.

"Don't forget what happened to the man who suddenly got everything he always wanted."

— Willy Wonka

"That's me, darling. Unusual places, unusual love affairs. I am a most strange and extraordinary person."

— Sally

⑳ Cabaret, 1972

Director: Bob Fosse
Runtime: 124 mins
Glamour factor: 4/5

Some of the musicals in this book have what could be described as adult themes; none more so than *Cabaret*, which is, incidentally, a genuine masterpiece of cinema. Inspired by the 1939 novel *Goodbye to Berlin* by Christopher Isherwood, *Cabaret* tells the story of Sally Bowles (Liza Minnelli), a young American in Berlin between the wars. Sally performs at the Kit Kat Klub and lives a free-spirited lifestyle. Brian Roberts (Michael York) arrives in Berlin to work on his doctorate and the two become friends and lovers, exploring the seedier side of the city's subculture.

Cabaret is a love story, but it also recounts the story of the end of innocence and freedom, its final big singing scene particularly menacing as the advent of Nazism is fully embraced.

Bob Fosse directed *Cabaret*, winning the Best Director Academy Award. Minnelli won Best Actress and the film scooped six more Oscars.

"Behold your shattered king!"

— Pontius Pilate

㉑ Jesus Christ Superstar, 1973

Director: Norman Jewison
Runtime: 106 mins
Glamour factor: 3/5

By the '70s, nothing was off the table in terms of inspiration for musical theatre, and Andrew Lloyd Webber and Tim Rice teamed up for a concept album based on the crucifixion of Jesus. Not the first subject you might think of, but the concept album became a rock opera, which in turn became a film.

Proving that the old stories are the best, *Jesus Christ Superstar* is genuinely gripping from start to finish. It is a tale of betrayal, love, lust and greed, and the lyrics and powerful songs drive it through to the inevitable conclusion.

Jesus (Ted Neeley), Mary Magdalene (Yvonne Elliman) and Judas (Carl Anderson) are the main characters, but Pontius Pilate (Barry Dennan) also features prominently. The cast perform with élan, many of the songs pushing their vocal skills to the limit. For a story we all know, *Jesus Christ Superstar* is tense and powerful.

㉒ The Rocky Horror Picture Show, 1975

Director: Jim Sharman
Runtime: 100 mins
Glamour factor: 5/5

This is a cult movie. Made only two years after the original stage production, *The Rocky Horror Picture Show* features many of the original cast members. It was written by Richard O'Brien, who plays Riff Raff, and is a glorious, glamorous, twisted homage to B-movies of the '50s, visually and musically.

Brad (Barry Bostwick) and Janet (Susan Sarandon) are stuck when their car breaks down and turn to Frank-N-Furter's castle for help. The plot is sexy, wacky and utterly hilarious. Watch out for Meat Loaf's spectacular entrance!

Way ahead of its time, *The Rocky Horror Picture Show* has been playing to packed, raucous audiences pretty much ever since it was released. The liberated, transsexual characters and freedom of expression sub-plots mark it out as truly original, and it is still supremely enjoyable some 50 years on.

“Don’t dream it, be it.”

— Dr Frank-N-Furter

㉓ Tommy, 1975

Director: Ken Russell
Runtime: 108 mins
Glamour factor: 3/5

Seminal rock band The Who engaged the services of flamboyant director Ken Russell (*Women in Love, The Devils*) for this dreamlike rock opera, so you can tell it is not going to be gentle.

Tommy (Roger Daltrey) is a teenager who witnessed a murder when he was young, and has been in a dissociated state ever since, unable to interact with people. It turns out that he's amazing at pinball, winning a championship game against the Pinball Wizard (Elton John) before "waking up". The story is convoluted and surreal, but the cast list reads like a who's who of '70s rock and cinema: Tina Turner, Eric Clapton, Arthur Brown, Oliver Reed, Paul Nicholas, Jack Nicholson and more.

Many of the songs are stunning and it is so "out there" that you will find there's genuinely nothing else like it.

"Your senses will never be the same."

— Film poster tag line

"It doesn't matter if you win or lose, it's what you do with your dancin' shoes."

— Vince Fontaine

㉔ Grease, 1978

Director: Randal Kleiser
Runtime: 110 mins
Glamour factor: 4/5

The '50s homage started in a slightly bizarre manner by *The Rocky Horror Picture Show* would take on a whole different tone just a couple of years later with the release of *Grease*. It was a huge mainstream success, catapulting the leads to fame and fortune.

Danny Zuko (John Travolta) and Sandy (Olivia Newton-John) enjoy a summer romance, and she returns to her native Australia at the end of it. Plot twist: who should be the new girl at Danny's school but Sandy herself, and Danny's school persona is not the one she fell for, so the two fall out. The rest of the movie is all about how they get back together, culminating in the huge final dance scene, 'We Go Together' (just after the previous huge dance scene: 'You're the One That I Want').

Grease is for everyone: the songs are endlessly singable, the characters lovable (even the baddies), and the staging is genius.

25 All That Jazz, 1979

Director: Bob Fosse
Runtime: 123 mins
Glamour factor: 4/5

Bob Fosse (*Cabaret*) was back for *All That Jazz*, a semi-autobiographical film based on parts of his long career in the industry.

Theatre director and choreographer Joe Gideon (Roy Scheider) goes through many trials and tribulations while trying to stage a new musical at the same time as editing a movie, not to mention trying to stay alive. He's not an easy man to work with or for, and it's not a pleasant experience for anyone concerned, Joe included.

All That Jazz mixes the real and imaginary with the surreal and dreamlike, making for a film that can be hard to watch at times, despite the entertaining aspects. This paradox is just one of the reasons this film was so well received; it won the Palme d'Or at the 1980 Cannes Film Festival, as well as four Academy Awards (from nine nominations).

"It's Show-time, folks!"

— Joe Gideon

"Can you tell me why you're so uptight about having your hair cut?"

— Prison psychiatrist

㉖ Hair, 1979

Director: Miloš Forman
Runtime: 121 mins
Glamour factor: 2/5

If culture reflects the politics of the time, then *Hair* is definitely an important film. Such wanton drug-taking, lewd behaviour and free love would give many conservative Americans a problem these days, so we can only imagine how the movie went down on first release.

Claude (John Savage) is about to be drafted to fight in Vietnam. En route, he meets a group of hippies, including George (Treat Williams) and Sheila (Beverly D'Angelo). Fascinated by the free-spirited (not to mention free-loving) nature of the group, he joins up with them. It ultimately ends in tears, but *Hair* does explore many issues that young Americans were protesting about throughout the '60s and '70s: segregation, class struggle, poverty and, above all, war.

Hair is an important part of movie counterculture. Between brilliant songs and scenes, important questions are asked.

27 Fame, 1980

Director: Alan Parker
Runtime: 133 mins
Glamour factor: 3/5

Fame the movie was just the beginning of what turned into a franchise, spawning multiple TV series, a stage show and even a remake movie in 2009.

Alongside *A Chorus Line* and *All That Jazz*, *Fame* explores the more realistic, hard-working side of show business. Set in New York's High School of Performing Arts (a real institution, although filming was not allowed to take place there), *Fame* follows a group of hopeful performers on their way through school. The characters, with problems in and out of the classroom, are well-rounded and believable, the performances superb, and the tension builds as the young people battle their way to graduation.

It is by no means a smooth ride, and the movie pulls no punches, but it is still a fan favourite – as is the classic 1982 TV series.

"Maybe I die undiscovered and my ghost gets the Grammy."

— Bruno Martelli

㉘ Little Shop of Horrors, 1980

Director: Frank Oz
Runtime: 94 mins
Glamour factor: 3/5

Once upon a time (1960) there was a film called *The Little Shop of Horrors*. It became a musical, which in turn became a film, directed by Frank Oz (of *The Muppets* fame).

Seymour (Rick Moranis) and Audrey (Ellen Greene) work in Mushnik's Flower Shop, which is failing. In a bid to prevent the store from closing, Seymour displays his own exotic plant, Audrey II (voiced by Levi Stubbs). He accidentally feeds it blood and the plant thrives. It turns out Audrey II can talk and needs human blood to survive...

Little Shop of Horrors is a bit of a hidden gem, sometimes forgotten in the shadow of its more famous contemporaries. But with its many catchy tunes, it is short, cute (it is a love story, after all) and great fun to watch.

"The guy sure looks like plant food to me."

— Seymour

㉙ Pennies From Heaven, 1981

Director: Herbert Ross
Runtime: 108 mins
Glamour factor: 3/5

There are not many musical movies that were adapted from surreal British TV series. *Pennies From Heaven* was just that, the original written by legendary television writer Dennis Potter. It was not an obvious choice for a movie but it worked, and it was even nominated for an Academy Award for Best Adapted Screenplay.

The story is dark and involves Arthur Parker (Steve Martin), a salesman in Chicago in the 1930s. He is married to Joan (Jessica Harper) but falls for the more exciting Eileen (Bernadette Peters). Mixing fantasy and reality and musical numbers from the era rather than new works, *Pennies From Heaven* is a strange film. A fascinating curiosity, it has hidden depths and is highly original.

"I've been putting it on every night, Arthur - hoping, praying that you'd come back to me."

— Joan Parker

"You love money and power and capitalism? You know they're never going to love you back."

— Grace

30 Annie, 1982

Director: John Huston
Runtime: 128 mins
Glamour factor: 2/5

Hollywood musicals took a bit of dark turn through the 1970s, but *Annie* brought the innocence and sunshine right back in!

Based on a comic strip, and set during the Great Depression, Annie (Aileen Quinn) lives in an orphanage run by the horribly cruel Agatha (Carol Burnett). Fortunately, millionaire Oliver Warbucks (Albert Finney) needs to improve his image so hires an orphan to live with him for a week. Annie wants nothing more than to find the parents who gave her up, and "Daddy" Warbucks is willing to help. So far so good, and it continues in wacky fashion to its conclusion.

Annie is a sweet film, with some highly memorable songs and plenty of hilarious, surreal shenanigans from the painfully cute lead. 'It's the Hard Knock Life' and 'Tomorrow' are truly songs for the ages.

"It is a moron who gives advice to a horse's arse."

— Waiter

㉛ Victor/Victoria, 1982

Director: Blake Edwards
Runtime: 132 mins
Glamour factor: 3/5

Musicals about singers and performers are common, as would be expected. Drawing on experiences, they are often autobiographical or factual. That, however, is not the case with *Victor/Victoria*, a fast-moving, hilarious farce.

Julie Andrews plays the title roles. Victoria is a down-at-heel American singer in Paris, who meets Toddy (Robert Preston), a gay man. After knocking out Toddy's ex-boyfriend, Toddy realizes Victoria could pass as a man. And as Count Victor Grazinski, a gay Polish female impersonator, she does just that, achieving the notoriety and success that eluded her as a woman. She draws the attention of supposed gangster King Marchand (James Garner). And that's just the start! Hidden identities and genders abound, but beneath the farce there are serious questions of acceptance and self-esteem. The expert Andrews excels in this odd role, making it an unforgettable film.

㉜ Evita, 1996

Director: Alan Parker
Runtime: 134 mins
Glamour factor: 4/5

The story of Evita Perón is a fascinating one, and was made into a musical in the '70s by stalwarts Tim Rice and Andrew Lloyd Webber. Their version was not filmed for another 20 years, and when it was, Hollywood put some serious resources behind it. The screenplay itself was written by Oliver Stone and Alan Parker, who also directed.

Madonna (Evita) and Antonio Banderas (Ché) lead an impressive cast as they tell the incredible, true, rags-to-riches story of the South American President's wife whose life and times caught the world's imagination.

Brits can only imagine Elaine Paige or Julie Covington in the big role (from the original musical), but Madonna does a very good job as the fascinating character. And freed from the constraints of a theatre, the movie is big in every way; a true epic.

"Don't cry for me Argentina."

— Evita Perón

“The greatest thing you’ll ever learn is just to love and be loved in return.”

— Christian

33 Moulin Rouge!, 2001

Director: Baz Luhrmann
Runtime: 128 mins
Glamour factor: 5/5

Moulin Rouge! is very much a Baz Luhrmann film. He co-wrote, produced and directed it, too; it is the realization of his vision. And what a vision it is – a beautiful love story from the early twentieth century, told through the medium of reimagined modern pop songs.

In Paris, Christian (Ewan Macgregor) is a writer who gets a job penning an extravagant musical to be put on at the Moulin Rouge. He meets courtesan and star of the show Satine (Nicole Kidman), who has been "promised" to the evil, rich Duke (Richard Roxburgh) in exchange for funding by the Moulin Rouge's unscrupulous owner (Jim Broadbent).

An absolute jaw-dropper from start to finish, *Moulin Rouge!* will leave you breathless and exhausted, with its combination of brilliantly realized music, extravagant staging and beautiful storyline.

34 Chicago, 2002

Director: Rob Marshall
Runtime: 113 mins
Glamour factor: 4/5

Musical movies have a long history of success at the Academy Awards, as Hollywood loves the medium. *Chicago* carried on that tradition, picking up six, including the coveted Best Picture. The original source material is a play from the 1920s, the golden age of gangsters, jazz – and murder.

The main characters are Roxie (Renée Zellweger) and Velma (Catherine Zeta-Jones), who meet on death row, having both killed their partners. The two become rivals, at once seeking fame and notoriety but also to be acquitted for the crimes they are accused of. The story may not sound glamorous, but *Chicago* is a high-octane hit, with a stream of superb song and dance routines and a cracking script. Performances from the stellar cast are amazing to match, making *Chicago* easily one of the all-time greats.

"This is Chicago, kid. You can't beat fresh blood on the walls."

— Billy Flynn

"If I am the phantom, it is because man's hatred has made me so."

— The Phantom

35 The Phantom of the Opera, 2004

Director: Joel Schumacher
Runtime: 143 mins
Glamour factor: 3/5

From the very first minutes, you'll feel a shiver down the spine, and when the famous riff starts you will be bewitched. By the end, you will be collapsed in your seat, wondering where the time went ... such is the power of the phantom.

More than just a film version of the hugely successful Andrew Lloyd Webber musical from 1986, *The Phantom of the Opera* includes all the great songs of the original, but makes the most of the medium of film to tell the haunting love story between the mysterious phantom and the object of his obsession, Christine Daaé (Emmy Rossum). There is plenty more going on in the Opera de Paris, and this extravagantly colourful film certainly draws the right attention to the glorious songs and sets.

36 Rent, 2005

Director: Chris Columbus
Runtime: 135 mins
Glamour factor: 1/5

A highly original look at the gritty lives of a group of New York individuals, *Rent* has proved to be highly influential, cited by Lin-Manuel Miranda as the inspiration that led him to write nontraditional musical theatre.

The characters in *Rent* are certainly unconventional, as are many of the themes, which involve the struggles of self-worth, identity and finance at the end of the '80s. Mark (Anthony Rapp) and Roger (Adam Pascal) are room-mates, and struggling (Mark with work as a film-maker, Roger with being HIV-positive). There are plenty of other interesting characters, including Mimi (Rosario Dawson), Maureen (Idina Menzell), Tom (Jesse L. Martin) and Angel (Wilson Jermaine Heredia).

The story is fascinating, challenging and bittersweet. However, it is ultimately uplifting and a really interesting piece of cinema.

"There are times when we're dirt broke, hungry and freezing, and I ask myself, why the hell am I still living here."

— Mark

㊲ Dreamgirls, 2006

Directors: Bill Condon
Runtime: 130 mins
Glamour factor: 4/5

This is not the story of Motown performers in any way; and certainly not the story of the Supremes. Or is it? Taking inspiration from that record company and that group, it does have much in common with both...

Curtis Taylor Jr (Jamie Foxx) is a record executive desperate to make a success of his latest group, the Dreams, with Black as well as white audiences in North America. Deena Jones (Beyoncé Knowles) is the lead singer who eventually marries him. Effie White (Jennifer Hudson) was previously the lead, and Curtis' lover, but his ruthless character is clear from the start. Lorrell Robinson (Anika Noni Rose) makes up the team.

Dreamgirls is the perfect mixture. The on-stage glamour and behind-the-scenes grit are combined expertly, and the outstanding cast and staging make a glittering spectacle.

"'Cause this time, Effie White's gonna win!"

— Effie Melody White

㊳ High School Musical, 2006

Director: Kenny Ortega
Runtime: 98 mins
Glamour factor: 4/5

Adults get their fair share of musicals, but what about the younger generation? *High School Musical* was just the first in a hugely popular series that hit all the right notes for millions of younger children. Although a made-for-TV movie, it delivers as much as many of its big-screen older siblings.

High School Musical tells the story of Troy (Zac Efron) and Gabriella (Vanessa Hudgens) who meet during a school break and then end up at the same school. Both great performers, they want to make it into the musical, but many obstacles stand in their way.

It's fun, it's frothy, it's lively and it's got tremendous energy. *High School Musical* is just right to watch with the kids, or if you need something to cheer yourself up and feel good about the world.

"My showerhead is very impressed with me."

— Troy Bolton

39 Hairspray, 2007

Director: Adam Shankman
Runtime: 116 mins
Glamour factor: 6/5

Hairspray is a musical movie based on *Hairspray* the musical, which was, in turn, based on the John Waters movie *Hairspray.* With such dilution you might think that quality would suffer, but that is far from the case.

It is the story of overweight teen Tracy Turnblad (Nikki Blonsky), who dreams of becoming a dancer on *The Corny Collins Show*. Suffice to say her dream comes true, but not without plenty of obstacles for Tracy and her friends to overcome. Not least of which is the sizeist, racist baddie Velma Von Tussle (Michelle Pfeiffer). In the original film, Tracy's mother was played by the divine Divine, here it is John Travolta – a long way from his usual roles.

Hairspray may have the sheen of simple teen movie, but underneath the colour and bubbles it is a charming, touching story of love, understanding and acceptance.

“I don’t want to be a laundress. I want to be famous.”

— Tracy Turnblad

"Somebody up there has got it in for me. I bet it's my mother."

— **Donna**

(40) Mamma Mia!, 2008

Director: Phyllida Lloyd
Runtime: 109 mins
Glamour factor: 3/5

In this list of Top 50 musical movies, we consciously avoided the "jukebox" movie, where an artist's songs are jammed together to make a story, of varying quality. However, Abba's output is so good, and the resulting film so effortlessly enjoyable, that *Mamma Mia!* more than earns its place.

Sophie (Amanda Seyfried) is about to get married. Her mother, Donna (Meryl Streep), has never told her which of three possibles her father is (Pierce Brosnan, Colin Firth, Stellan Skarsgård), so Sophie invites them all to the wedding, without telling her mother.

There's not much depth to the proceedings, but you can tell the cast are having an absolute ball and it's infectious – even the grumpiest will be tapping their feet and singing along by the end.

"Fight. Dream. Hope. Love."

— Film poster tag line

41 Les Misérables, 2012

Director: Tom Hooper
Runtime: 158 mins
Glamour factor: 3/5

Victor Hugo, upon first publication of *Les Misérables* in 1862, could never have imagined the effect his book would have on popular culture more than 130 years later. What this highlights is the sheer quality of the story and the power of the characters he wrote all those years ago.

It is 1815 in France, and Jean Valjean (Hugh Jackman) is released on parole from prison, where he has served 19 years for stealing some bread to feed a starving child. Years later he turns up as a factory owner and one of his workers, Fantine (Ann Hathaway), is sacked unfairly. Fantine dies, but Valjean swears to look after her daughter, Cosette (Amanda Seyfried). Marius (Eddie Redmayne) is her love interest, but most of the story is concerned with misery, failed revolution and heartache. Highlights from the all-star cast include Sacha Baron Cohen and Helena Bonham Carter as the dreadful Thenardiers.

㊷ La La Land, 2016

Director: Damien Chazelle
Runtime: 128 mins
Glamour factor: 5/5

The Award for Best Picture went to ... *La La Land*, but only for two minutes. That famous gaffe notwithstanding, the movie could easily have won that prize, as it did many others.

Seb Wilder (Ryan Gosling) meets Mia (Emma Stone) in LA. He's an aspiring musician, she's an aspiring actress. Eventually, they become involved romantically, before breaking up when his star is on the rise. Years later, her star is risen fully and the two meet by chance.

The premise is simple: boy meets girl, they fall in love, they split. But *La La Land* is an absolutely beautiful, believable love story that's filled with stunning, surreal numbers and a lovely, realistic message. Inspired heavily by *Les Parapluies de Cherbourg* (*see page 44*), it is a truly touching story that oozes class from every frame.

"People love what other people are passionate about."

— Mia

"No one ever made a difference by being like everyone else."

43 The Greatest Showman, 2017

Director: Michael Gracey
Runtime: 105 mins
Glamour factor: 3/5

Barnstorming, brilliant family entertainment, *The Greatest Showman* is a joy to watch from start to finish. It has love, laughter, tears, joy and surprise in equal measure.

P. T. Barnum (Hugh Jackman) is an entrepreneur who marries childhood sweetheart Charity (Michelle Williams), against her parents' wishes. He opens a museum but is on the verge of failure until he introduces some live "freak" performers. He aspires to bigger things, touring with the famous Swedish singer Jenny Lind (Rebecca Ferguson), to mixed results, especially when it comes to affairs of the heart. A side romance is that of Phillip Carlyle (Zac Efron) and Anne Wheeler (Zendaya).

The music is absolutely sublime, an endless line of memorable hits, and the staging excellent: it's the greatest show, man.

(44) A Star is Born, 2018

Director: Bradley Cooper
Runtime: 136 mins
Glamour factor: 4/5

The tale is pretty familiar by now, and has been made four times in Hollywood. An older, fading male star meets an up-and-coming performer. Her star is rising; his is fading; it all ends in tragedy.

In 1937 it was Janet Gaynor and Fredric March, in 1954 Judy Garland and James Mason, in 1976 Barbra Streisand and Kris Kristofferson, and the 2018 version featured Lady Gaga and Bradley Cooper. Each film is very good – probably because of the tragic, timeless nature of the material – and all are very much worth watching, although maybe not one after the other.

The 2018 version was expertly directed by Cooper, too, and Lady Gaga won multiple awards for her scintillating performance.

"I hope it's okay if I love you forever."

— Ally Maine

"Real love's hard to come by. So you find a way to cope without it."

— Elton John

㊺ Rocketman, 2019

Director: Dexter Fletcher
Runtime: 121 mins
Glamour factor: 4/5

There are not many jukebox musicals on this list. But *Rocketman* is not a regular jukebox movie, it is more like a fantastic reimagining of the early years of seminal rock star Elton John's career.

Taron Egerton excels in the part of Elton, and his singing voice is stunning. In fact, the cast is brilliant and the big scenes worthy of the glamorous star we know Elton to be. Every song was re-recorded for the film, making the soundtrack highly original.

With a number of surreal sequences and some gritty content, *Rocketman* is not like any other biographical movie you might see. But when it comes to Elton John, you would not expect it any other way.

㊻ Hamilton, 2020

Director: Thomas Kail
Runtime: 160 mins
Glamour factor: 3/5

I know it's "only" the filmed version of the Broadway show, but that does not make *Hamilton* the movie any less good. Or relevant. Or anything other than utterly brilliant. You can tell we are fans.

The story of founding father Alexander Hamilton is told in two acts, from his arrival on the political scene in 1776 to his death by gunshot wound 24 years later. The backdrop is the establishment of the United States as a single, independent country. In case you did not know, the cast of *Hamilton* are almost all non-white actors, and the music is overwhelmingly hip hop, R&B, soul and pop. It is a clever, relevant way of telling a story that is still unfolding, even today. A one-man music machine, Lin-Manuel Miranda wrote the lyrics, composed the music and also played Hamilton himself. He certainly did not throw away his shot!

"I am not throwing away my shot."

— Alexander Hamilton

47 Dear Evan Hansen, 2021

Director: Stephen Chbosky
Runtime: 137 mins
Glamour factor: 3/5

This is a modern movie with a very modern message. *Dear Evan Hansen* deals with difficult topics in an honest, touching way, and is an uplifting, moving film.

Evan Hansen (Ben Platt) is a teenager with anxiety issues. His therapist suggests he writes a letter to himself ('Dear Evan Hansen') every day. One of the letters is found by his classmate Connor Murphy (Colton Ryan), who kills himself shortly afterwards. Connor's parents misunderstand the letter, thinking it was written by their son, and they develop a friendship with Evan, who is also in love with their daughter, Zoe (Kaitlyn Dever). Accidental and deliberate lies, loneliness and longing fill the story, which is sad and serious, but ultimately positive.

A musical with a conscience, *Dear Evan Hansen* asks valid questions, and does its best to answer them in a mature, caring manner.

"You will be found."

— Evan Hansen

㊽ In the Heights, 2021

Director: Jon M. Chu
Runtime: 143 mins
Glamour factor: 3/5

If you ever thought New York City was an exciting, noisy place to live or visit, *In the Heights* will have you reaching out to your travel agent. It is a busy, bustling blast of a movie, and a moving homage to the city's latinx population.

Usnavi (Anthony Ramos) recounts a love story to some children. He runs a shop in Washington Heights, home to a large Dominican community including his crush, Vanessa (Melissa Barrera). But the area is changing, and change brings problems...

In the Heights crackles with energy, each number building brilliantly upon the last. Some are homely, others are spectacular. There is humour, tension, emotion and simply amazing singing and dancing. Lin-Manuel does it again!

"Ignore anyone who doubts you."

— Kevin Rosario

"I'm not afraid. It's the Wizard who should be afraid of me."

— Elphaba

㊾ Wicked, Part 1, 2024

Director: Jon M. Chu
Runtime: 160 mins
Glamour factor: 4/5

What do you get if you spin off from *The Wizard of Oz*? If anyone answered *The Wiz*, yes you get a point but that's not what we're after. What we want is *Wicked*, the movie version of the hugely popular stage show.

Glinda the Good (Ariana Grande) celebrates the death of the Wicked Witch of the West, but then opts to tell the witch's back story, that of her former friend Elphaba Thropp (Cynthia Erivo). A magical but all-to-real story it is, with shattered dreams, lost loves, misunderstanding and treachery.

Wicked was a massive critical and popular success across the world, receiving ten Academy Award nominations (winning two: Best Costume Design and Best Production Design) and countless other gongs.

50 Emilia Perez, 2024

Director: Jacques Audiard
Runtime: 132 mins
Glamour factor: 4/5

It is fitting that the last musical in this book is an extraordinary one, groundbreaking and utterly original, with a score to match.

Rita (Zoe Saldaña) is an unscrupulous lawyer in Mexico City who is employed by the powerful cartel boss Manitas (Karla Sofía Gascón) to do all the groundwork for him to undergo gender reassignment surgery after faking his own death. (I know, not your usual musicals subject matter.) Everything goes as planned and Manitas becomes Emilia. Years later, however, Emilia decides to be reunited with Manitas' wife Jessi (Selena Gomez) and children, so pretends to be a distant cousin welcoming them back to Mexico City.

The serious storyline (Emilia tries to atone for the sins of Manitas) and haunting songs make for a stunning film, and the tense, exciting finale will leave you breathless.

"This isn't an escape; it's a rebirth."

— Emilia

BEHIND THE CAMERA

Richard Rodgers (1902–1979) & Oscar Hammerstein II (1895–1960)

The two worked together on some of the most popular musicals ever made, including *Oklahoma!*, *Carousel*, *State Fair*, *The King and I* and *The Sound of Music*. Rodgers was the composer and Hammerstein the lyricist. Together they made an incredible team, with no loss of quality over the decades of work.

Vincente Minnelli (1903–1986)

A stage and film director, Minnelli is probably most famous for directing the musical movies *Meet Me in St. Louis* (where he first met wife-to-be Judy Garland), *An American in Paris* and *Gigi*. Father of Liza Minnelli (with Garland), he directed a number of other films and various plays. He was the set and costume designer for *Ziegfeld Follies of 1936*.

Gene Kelly (1912–1996)

An absolutely amazing dancer in his own right, Kelly was also a singer, actor, director and choreographer. Without a doubt of the all-time musical greats, he was an innovative performer and director, making popular films such as *On the Town* and *Singin' in the Rain* (which he wrote, directed and choreographed, see page 22), as well as *Brigadoon*, *It's Always Fair Weather*, *Invitation to the Dance* and countless others.

Robert Wise (1914–2005)

A legend in the business, Wise was the man who directed *West Side Story* and *The Sound of Music* for the big screen. He worked as an editor of the Orson Welles classic *Citizen Kane* and was also a producer (*Return to Paradise, West Side Story, The Sound of Music,* etc.) and executive producer. He won Academy Awards for both of his big musicals, in 1961 and 1965, respectively.

"Dance expresses joy better than anything else."

— Bob Fosse

Bob Fosse (1927–1987)

A dancer, choreographer and director, Fosse was a hugely important figure in the evolution of musical theatre on the big screen, often associated with a harder, darker side of the genre. His most famous work is directing *Cabaret* (winner of the Academy Award for Best Picture) and *All That Jazz* (winner of the Palme d'Or), but his work as a choreographer is probably even more influential, with jazz dance his speciality.

Jon M. Chu (1979)

One of the youngest directors in this book, Jon M. Chu had a breakthrough as director of *Crazy Rich Asians*, a global hit. He had already directed two dance movies, *Step Up 2: The Streets* and *Step Up 3D*. His next two movies were musicals: *In the Heights* and *Wicked*; with such great films already behind him, further success is sure!

Lin-Manuel Miranda (1980)

A hugely talented songwriter, actor and singer, Miranda is probably best known for the Broadway musical *Hamilton*, but he also wrote songs and music for the incredibly popular Disney movies *Moana* and *Encanto*. He is proud of his Puerto Rican origins, and this, and other interesting themes are very prominent in his work.

"Everyone deserves the chance to fly!"

— Elphaba,
***Wicked*, 2024**